# PIRANHAS

Deborah Chancellor

**Smart Apple Media**

Smart Apple Media is published by Black Rabbit Books
P.O. Box 3263, Mankato, Minnesota 56002

Printed in the United States

Published by arrangement with the Watts Publishing Group Ltd, London.

Editors: Rachel Tonkin and Julia Bird
Designer: Proof Books
Picture researcher: Diana Morris

Picture credits:
Amazon Images/Alamy: front cover, 1; George Bernard/NHPA: 25; blickwinkel/Schmidbauer/Alamy: 7; Comstock/Corbis: 10; Lee Dalton/NHPA: 8; Max Gibbs/OSF: 27; Neil Hepworth/Alamy: 11; Roger Jackman/OSF: 22; Johnny Jensen/JJPhoto.dk: 9; Trevor McDonald/NHPA: 29; John Madere/Corbis: 23; Hugh Maynard/Nature PL: 15; Alf Jacob Nilsen/Biophoto/PD: 6; Pegaz/Alamy: 4; Kevin Schafer/Corbis: 13; Michal Setka/PD: 28; Robert Slade/Alamy: 21; Trevor Smithies/Alamy: 5. Sunset_Paris/A1 Pix : 17.

All other photography: Andy Crawford

With thanks to Woodford Aquatics

Library of Congress Cataloging-in-Publication Data

Chancellor, Deborah.
        Piranhas / Deborah Chancellor.
        p. cm.—(Smart Apple Media. Extreme pets)
        Summary: "Advice for kids on how to choose and care for several common breeds of piranhas, including tank setup, feeding, and keeping piranhas healthy"—Provided by publisher.
        Includes index.
        ISBN-13: 978-1-59920-237-2
        1. Piranhas—Juvenile literature.  I. Title.
SF458.P57C43 2009
639.3'748—dc22

                                                                                2007035384

9 8 7 6 5 4 3 2 1

# Contents

# What Are Piranhas?

Piranhas are freshwater fish that live in the rivers of the Amazon rainforest in South America. People think of piranhas as fierce meat-eaters. However, some piranha species are harmless vegetarians.

## Piranhas As Pets

Piranhas can be kept as pets in a home aquarium. They are fast swimmers, capable of impressive twists and turns in the water. Although they are not exactly pretty, their strength and speed makes them fascinating to watch. Keeping piranhas can be a challenging hobby, but it is becoming increasingly popular.

**Piranhas are famous members of the family of fish known as characins, or tetras.**

## Feeding Frenzy

In the wild, piranhas have a reputation for attacking in big schools, stripping large animals of flesh in bloody feeding frenzies. This can be true of a few species of piranhas, particularly during the dry season when food is scarce. But it is exaggerated. Piranhas are unlikely to attack large animals unless the animals are already injured or bleeding. Meat-eating piranhas mostly survive on fish, bugs, and small river creatures.

## Breeding Piranhas

Female piranhas lay eggs in a nest among river plants. Both parents then guard the nest. The eggs hatch after two or three days, and a few days later the baby fish, called fry, are able to swim independently. Young piranhas find food and shelter in riverbank vegetation until they are big enough to hunt in open water.

# Big Teeth

Piranhas have razor-sharp teeth and powerful jaws. Triangular teeth in the fish's upper and lower jaws lock together like a trap. The teeth are so interlocked that piranhas don't lose teeth individually—they lose a whole row at once. A new row quickly grows back to replace the old one.

## Jaws of Steel

Piranhas' teeth are so sharp that they have been known to bite through metal fishing hooks!

# Living with Piranhas

The native peoples of the Amazon rainforest swim and fish in rivers where piranhas are known to live and only very rarely are attacked. In fact, piranhas are the ones more likely to come to harm, because their meat is a staple part of the native Amazonians' diet.

# Questions & Answers

✳ **Where do piranhas live in the wild?**
Piranhas live in the Amazon River and smaller rivers that flow into it. The Amazon River stretches for 4,163 miles (6,700 km) across South America, flowing out into the Atlantic Ocean. It contains 20 percent of all the Earth's river water.

✳ **How many species of piranha are there?**
Estimates vary, but there are about 20 main species of piranha.

✳ **Can piranhas kill people?**
There is no known case of a person being killed by a piranha. However, piranhas can be dangerous if they are frightened or hungry. They may bite and can cause a painful injury.

In the Amazon rainforest, the native people catch piranhas to eat and make tools from their sharp teeth.

# Red-Bellied Piranhas

There are two main groups of piranhas, the pygocentrus and the serrasalmus groups. Piranhas in the pygocentrus group all have blunt, "bulldog" type faces. The red-bellied piranha belongs to the pygocentrus group.

A school of red-bellied piranhas should get along well together.

## Starter Piranha

The red-bellied piranha (*Pygocentrus nattereri*) is the species of piranha most commonly kept as a pet. It is a good species to start off with if you are new to keeping piranhas. Red-bellies are hardy fish that can survive a variety of water conditions. However, like all piranhas, this fish should be cared for with extreme caution, because it can be quite aggressive.

## Safety in Numbers

The red-bellied piranha can be kept in small schools—it is best to keep at least four of them together in one tank. A smaller number is not a good idea. One fish will quickly become dominant and may become aggressive toward its tank mates.

## Pretty As a Piranha

Young red-bellied piranhas are a blue-grey color with olive-green sides. Their bodies sparkle as they catch the light. This fish is named after the startling red color of its belly. As red-bellied piranhas get older, their colors begin to fade.

# Orinoco Red-Bellied Piranha

The Orinoco red-bellied piranha (*Pygocentrus cariba*) is a close relative of the red-bellied piranha. Both fish grow to the same size and have a similarly fierce appearance. It is easy to tell them apart however, because the Orinoco red-bellied piranha has a big black spot on its side. It is also more active than its relative. Be very careful if you need to move this fish.

## Adult Size

The red-bellied piranha grows up to 12 inches (30 cm) long and weighs up to 8 pounds(3.5 kg).

## Questions & Answers

* **Why is the red-bellied piranha the most commonly kept species?**
The red-bellied piranha has been bred successfully outside South America, so it is easily available at a reasonable cost.

* **Where can I get a red-bellied piranha?**
Red-bellies are now widely bred in captivity in the United States and are also available from good pet shops or aquarium stores.

* **Why are some piranha species unavailable in the U.S.?**
Some species are rarely found in the U.S. because they are not bred outside South America, and it is difficult to transport them from the wild.

# King of Piranhas

Another piranha in this group is the piraya (*Pygocentrus piraya*), sometimes known as the "king of the piranhas." It is one of the most attractive piranhas, with a bright orange belly and tufted fins. However, this is not a species for children or beginners. This big fish can grow to over 20 inches (50 cm) long and needs lots of food to satisfy its big appetite. A hungry piraya will become violent toward anything that moves.

Piraya require a large tank to swim in.

# Black, Red-Throated, and Pike Piranhas

The black piranha (*Serrasalmus rhombeus*) is a famous member of the serrasalmus group of piranhas. The fish in this group have different features than their pygocentrus cousins. Their faces are longer and narrower, and their bodies are more streamlined. This means that they can swim faster after their prey.

## Lone Fish

The black piranha is bigger and much more aggressive than the red-bellied piranha. It is a solitary fish that likes to guard its territory—if it is kept in a school, individuals will attack and kill each other. For this reason, black piranhas should be kept on their own in a large tank.

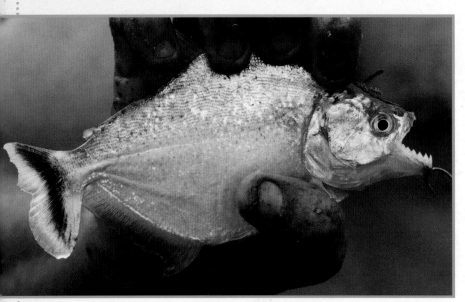

A young black piranha shows off its sharp teeth.

## Take Care

The black piranha is the most dangerous of the serrasalmus group of piranhas. It is not advisable to keep this piranha as a pet—a fully-grown black piranha could bite off a human hand in two or three bites. If you do decide to keep a black piranha, you should make sure that you have help from an experienced adult piranha keeper.

## Changing Color

Young black piranhas are pale in color. For this reason, they are sometimes called "white piranhas," which can be confusing. Adult black piranhas are darker in color, and their eyes go blood-red as they get older.

# Red-Throated Piranha

The red-throated piranha (*Serrasalmus spilopleura*) is smaller and less fierce than its relative, the black piranha. It can be kept in small schools, but it does have a tendency to attack the fins of its tank mates. In the rivers of the Amazon rainforest, this species of piranha feeds mainly on fins and scales of other fish. It can grow up to 8 inches (20 cm) long.

## Keen Senses

Piranhas have excellent senses of smell and hearing, which help them find food in murky water. They can actually see more colors than humans!

# Questions & Answers

* **Is the black piranha a cannibal?**
  Yes. Like many other species of piranha, the black piranha will attack, kill, and eat its own kind. However, it will only do this when its territory is threatened, or when it is hungry.

* **How are serrasalmus and pygocentrus piranhas different?**
  The fish in these two groups are different in appearance (see page 8). Pygocentrus piranhas are also more content in schools, while serrasalmus piranhas should usually be kept separately. However, both species are aggressive meat-eaters.

# Pike Piranha

The pike piranha (*Serrasalmus elongatus*) is another member of the serrasalmus group. This fish is not often kept as a pet. If it is, it must be kept on its own or it will attack its companions. It is built for speed, with a slim body up to 8.7 inches (22 cm) long. In the wild, this fish chases and ambushes prey from behind, stripping the flesh with its long rows of sharp teeth.

Pike piranhas are fierce predators in their natural habitat.

# Keeping Piranhas

Caring for piranhas can be very rewarding. These amazing fish are fascinating to watch in an aquarium. However, you need to think carefully before you decide to keep piranhas. You must have the support of an adult in your family, because piranhas are expensive pets and can be dangerous.

## Do Your Homework

Before you set up a piranha aquarium, find out as much as you can about piranhas and how to care for them. Buy books, and look at some good aquarium Web sites (see page 31). Look up a local vet or fish expert who can give you advice. It is vital that you and your family know what you are taking on before you buy any equipment or fish.

## Big Responsibility

If you want to keep piranhas, you must be prepared to care for them properly. You will need to give them enough space to swim with plenty of hiding places. Your piranhas will need clean, warm water and a varied diet. Caring for your fish will take time and cost money. Remember that some species of piranhas can live for many years (see page 11).

**Make sure you do plenty of research before you decide to buy a piranha.**

## Piranha Sitter

Piranhas are not everybody's idea of a "cute" pet. It may be hard to find someone to care for your fish when your family is on vacation. You will have to find someone who is prepared to take on this responsibility before you buy your piranhas.

# Count the Cost

Keeping piranhas is an expensive hobby. Talk about it with your family. Make sure you can afford all the equipment that you will need, as well as the ongoing food and vet bills.

## Piranha Ban

Keeping piranhas is illegal in many U.S. states. In warmer climates, piranhas would take over all freshwater life forms if they were released into local water systems!

## Check Your House

You must be sure that you have enough space in your home for your aquarium. Piranhas need very big tanks, which are very heavy when full of water. You will need to be sure that the floor of your home is strong enough to hold the weight of a full tank.

# Questions & Answers

✳ **How long do piranhas live?**
Different species live for different lengths of time—anything between four and fifteen years depending on the species and the quality of care that they get.

✳ **How big should my tank be?**
You will need at least 2.5 gallons (9 liters) of water for every inch (2.5 cm) of adult fish length. A school of four red-bellied piranhas will need an aquarium of at least 48 inches x 18 inches x 18 inches (122 cm x 46 cm x 46 cm). It is best to get a tank this big right away.

✳ **What if I need to find a new home for my piranhas?**
If the unexpected happens (e.g. you have to move to a smaller house), then either find a piranha keeper who will take your fish, or have them put to sleep by a vet. Never release piranhas into a river or any other body of water.

A well-kept aquarium can look very attractive but takes up a lot of space!

# Choosing the Right Tank

The most essential piece of equipment for keeping piranhas is a good quality tank. You should buy the biggest tank you have room for and can afford. Your tank should be watertight, sturdy, and non-toxic. It can be made of either glass or acrylic.

## Think Ahead

Figure out how big your tank should be according to how large your fish will grow and how many of them you want to keep. You should allow a minimum of 18 to 23 gallons (70–90 l) of water per fish. Choose a tank that is big enough for adult piranhas. It is cruel to keep any fish in a tank that is too small. Overcrowding will make the tank dirtier and harder to maintain, and will make your fish ill.

## Tank Stand

You will need a stand to put your tank on. Water weighs about 22 pounds (1 kg) a liter so your stand will need to be very strong to support a full aquarium. Make sure the base of the stand is level. If an aquarium is not absolutely horizontal, it may develop stresses and start to leak.

## Location, Location

It is important to find the right place in your home for your tank. You will need a large space that is close to sources of water and electricity. The corner of a downstairs room is probably best, where the floor is strongest to bear the weight of a full tank.

Aquarium centers and pet shops sell good tank stands, like this sturdy stand with cabinet space for equipment.

## Tank Top

Your tank will also need a top. This will stop your piranha from jumping out and reduce evaporation from the tank. It will also contain the lighting for your tank and may hold other equipment, such as air pumps or fans.

## Growing Pains

It is a myth that fish never outgrow their tanks. Piranhas can grow very quickly and will get stressed if they don't have enough space.

## Growing Fish

If red-bellied piranhas are kept in the right-sized tank in the correct conditions, they should grow up to 6 inches (15 cm) long in their first year. After this, they will grow up to 1 inch (2.5 cm) per year until they reach their full adult length of about 12 inches (30 cm).

## Questions & Answers

* **Should I get a glass or an acrylic tank?**
Glass tanks are heavier and more fragile than acrylic tanks, but they are also clearer to look through, harder to scratch, and less expensive.

* **What if I can't fit a big tank in my home?**
Some species of piranhas are smaller and are happy to be housed alone. These include *Serrasalmus sanchezi, Serrasalmus irritan,* and *Serrasalmus maculatus.*

* **What if my local pet store doesn't sell big tanks?**
If your pet store is a good one, it should be able to place a special order for the tank you want.

The bigger your tank, the more naturally your fish will behave and the quicker they will grow to adult size, like this red-bellied piranha.

# Heaters and Filters

Heaters and filters are important pieces of equipment for keeping piranhas. In the wild, these fish swim in warm waters. They will not survive in an aquarium if they are kept in cold water. Your piranhas also need their water to be properly filtered, so that waste in the tank is processed to become less harmful.

## Power Filter

One of the strongest and most effective filtration systems is the power filter. This cleans waste from the water by siphoning it up from the tank and passing it through a filter (usually some kind of sponge), before returning the clean water to the tank. Most power filters can also be set to treat the tank water with cleaning chemicals.

A power filter will help keep your piranha aquarium clean.

## Under-Gravel Filter

Under-gravel filters work by drawing the water from the tank down through a gravel substrate (floor covering). Place this kind of filter at the bottom of your tank, laying up to 2 inches (5 cm) of coarse gravel on top of it. Slope the gravel down to the front of the tank to make it easier to clean. Don't use very fine gravel, or it will clog up your filter.

## Biological Filter

Natural bacteria and other microorganisms in your tank help convert fish waste into less toxic substances. This is called biological filtration and is established in the first two months of keeping an aquarium. The process of starting up a biological filter is called "cycling" (see page 19).

# Hot Water

You will need an aquarium heater and thermostat to keep your tank water at the right temperature for your pets. Use an aquarium thermometer to check the temperature. Try to use it every time you feed your fish. Any big change in temperature will be harmful and needs to be fixed immediately.

## Safety Warning

Never forget that electricity and water are a very dangerous mix. Always unplug all electrical aquarium equipment before it is serviced and checked.

**Keep your water warm and make sure it circulates around the tank to mimic your piranha's natural environment in the fast-flowing Amazon River.**

## Questions & Answers

* **How warm should my tank water be?**
  Your piranha's tank water should always be between 76°F and 82°F (24 and 28°C).

* **How many filters and heaters do I need?**
  Use more than one heater and filter in case either of them stop working. Use at least two smaller heaters to provide the same power as one big one, and do the same for your filters.

## Air Pumps

The water in your piranha tank must have enough oxygen in it to keep your fish healthy. Check with an expert to see whether your tank's filter creates enough oxygen. If not, you will need to install an air pump to boost the oxygen in the tank.

# Decorations and Lighting

It is best to keep piranhas in a dimly lit, well-decorated tank. Piranhas like to have plenty of hiding places. Some species, such as the red-bellied piranha, are nervous and may swim away when you go near their tank. They will get stressed if they don't have enough shelter to hide in.

## Make It Real

Choose your tank decorations carefully to create a natural-looking environment. Use hard rocks, bogwood logs, and plants. When you arrange your decorations, put tall plants at the back to hide tank equipment and make it easier to see your fish swimming in front of them. Black gravel substrate (floor covering) on the tank bed will complement the colors of most piranhas.

Try to find decorations that will create a realistic "Amazon" setting in your aquarium.

## Plants for Piranhas

Most piranhas eat plants and will graze on any vegetation you provide. Floating plants look good in the tank and can also help dim your lighting levels. However, artificial plants are easier to care for than real ones and often look very realistic.

## Decoration "Don'ts"

Never decorate your aquarium with shells, corals, or soft rocks like limestone. All of these can contain chemicals that are bad for your fish. Use a gravel substrate rather than rocks, since rocks won't provide enough cover for your fish. Avoid rocks with sharp edges, as they may injure your fish.

Aquarium plants make your tank look attractive and provide plenty of cover for your fish.

## Dim Light

In the wild, piranhas swim in murky rivers. Piranhas do like the dark, but you will want to be able to see your fish in their aquarium. Light your tank dimly, using aquarium fluorescent tubes with "daylight"-type bulbs. These will fit into the lid of your tank. Your piranhas will get used to the light, as long as it isn't too bright.

## Places to Hide

Half to three quarters of the floor space in your tank should contain hiding places.

## Day and Night

Ask an adult to help you set up a timer switch on your lighting to create a cycle of day and night. Your fish should have 12 hours of light followed by 12 hours of darkness. This cycle is good for your piranhas, as well as for any live plants in your aquarium.

## Questions & Answers

✳ **Will I ever see my piranhas if I give them lots of places to hide?**
Yes. The more shelter your fish have, the more confident and less stressed they will be. They will spend more time swimming in open space where you can see them.

✳ **How will I know if my tank is too brightly lit?**
Piranhas don't like bright light and find it uncomfortable. If your tank is too bright, your piranhas will swim around quickly in an agitated way.

✳ **Can I put ornaments in my tank to decorate it?**
You should decorate your tank with ornaments from an aquarium shop. Other "found" objects may contain chemicals that dissolve in water and could poison your fish. Always rinse new decorations before you put them in your tank.

# Setting up Your Aquarium

It will take a day or two to get your aquarium ready for your piranhas. First of all, lift your empty tank onto its stand. Then take the following steps to prepare your aquarium. Always get an adult to help you, and remember to be careful with electricity— never turn on or check equipment with wet hands.

## Step 1: Filters

If you are using an under–gravel filter, place it at the bottom of the tank, and cover it with 2 inches (5 cm) of coarse gravel. Position your filters inside or outside the tank, depending on what type of filter you have. You will need to follow the installation instructions that come with your filtration equipment.

## Step 2: Decorations

Arrange your decorations carefully in the tank. If you are putting in any big rocks or plants, anchor them securely under the gravel so they don't topple over with the water currents. If you are using bogwood decorations, make sure you soak them in water first so they don't float up to the surface.

**Aquarium gravel comes in a variety of different sizes and colors.**

## Step 3: Water

Fill the tank with tap water. Don't fill it right up to the brim, because your fish need to get oxygen from air above the surface. Then, add chlorine or chloramine remover to the water. You can buy this in droplet form from aquarium shops. Always follow the instructions and ask an adult to help you.

## Step 4: Heating and Lighting

When you install your heating equipment, let it sit in the full tank for at least half an hour before you turn it on. This will stop sudden heat from splitting the tank. Put the tank lid on and check that the lighting works. Now let your tank run for two days to make sure everything is working. The water must be at the right temperature (see page 15) before you add your piranhas.

## Step 5: Cycling Your Tank

Natural bacteria help filter your tank water. They are established in the first four to eight weeks after you set up your aquarium. This process is called "cycling." When you first put your piranhas in the tank, change around 15 to 20 percent of the water every other day (see page 24). Always dechlorinate new water before you add it. After about eight weeks, your "biological filter" should be working. From then on, only do water changes once a week.

To fill your tank, pour the water carefully onto a dish or saucer so you don't disturb the gravel and decorations.

## Questions & Answers

✴ **What happens if the water temperature is wrong?**
If your tank water is too hot, your fish will not have enough oxygen, which will cause nerve and heart damage. If the water is too cold, it may damage your piranhas' immune systems.

✴ **Why do I need to dechlorinate the water?**
Chlorine and chloramine are chemicals that are added to tap water to clean it for humans to use. These chemicals are dangerous for your fish.

✴ **Why do I need to cycle my tank?**
You must cycle your tank to create a natural "biological filter." This will help break down poisonous waste that would be harmful to your piranhas.

# Buying Your Piranhas

Go to a good pet shop or aquarium center to buy your piranhas. If possible, ask someone who owns piranhas to recommend a store to you. If you can, try to find a small pet shop, not a big chain store. The products and service will usually be better, and the staff will know more about piranhas.

## How Many Piranhas?

Get expert advice on how many piranhas to buy. This will depend on the species you want to keep, because some piranhas should be housed alone, and others can be kept in schools (see pages 6–9). If you want a school of piranhas, they need to all be from the same species and should be around the same size.

## Healthy Fish

Never buy a piranha that looks sick or is in a tank with others that look sick. Even if your chosen piranha seems well, it may be carrying the same disease as its tank mates. Watch out for thin or sluggish fish and unusual marks on their bodies. If the water is an odd color it may be medicated and the fish may be unhealthy.

Ask for lots of advice when you buy your piranhas. The staff at a good pet shop should be willing and able to help you.

Make sure you chose a healthy piranha, or your fish may not live long when you get it home.

## Grumpy Old Fish

Some piranhas are happy in schools when they are young. When they get older they become more solitary and may attack their tank mates.

## Questions & Answers

✳ **Is it best to buy young piranhas?**
Yes. They will live longer, and adapt better to life together in a school. Introduce them into your tank at the same time, and let them grow up together.

✳ **Can I add new fish to an established group?**
If you have to do this, do it carefully, preferably after feeding time and when the lighting is off, so that your piranhas are relaxed and not aggressively active. Your new piranha should be of the same size and species as those already in the tank.

✳ **Can I keep different species of piranhas together?**
Generally, this is a bad idea. Big piranhas will attack smaller, weaker species.

## Bringing Piranhas Home

Always transport piranhas individually. The stress of movement could make them attack each other. If the journey is short, you can transport your fish in buckets with lids, but make sure you use new plastic buckets that have not been used for cleaning first. If your journey home is a long one, ask a member of the staff in the pet shop to put your piranhas in a perforated plastic container with a lid inside a large, strong, and sealed bag of water. This will stop your fish from biting through the bag on the way home. When you get home, ask an adult to help transfer your piranhas into your tank with a long-handled aquarium net.

## Putting Piranhas in Your Tank

Never mix the water your piranhas have traveled in with your home tank water. This can introduce disease into your tank. If your piranhas are in bags, let each unopened bag float in your tank for about 20 minutes. Open the bags and get an adult to add some water from the tank into them, and close them up again. Let them float for another 20 minutes. Then the piranhas can be netted out of the bags and put into the tank. In this way, the piranhas get used to the temperature of the new tank water, but no shop water is introduced into the tank.

# Feeding Your Piranhas

Most piranhas are omnivores, which means that they eat both meat and plants. They need a varied diet. The more variety you offer your fish, the less likely it is that one type of food will become a health problem. A good, diverse diet will also prevent your piranhas from losing interest in food.

A piranha uses its sharp teeth to crack the nuts and berries that fall into the waters of the Amazon River.

## Piranha Food

You can offer many types of food to your piranhas—fresh, frozen, freeze-dried, and canned. Fresh foods include raw meat and vegetables. Suitable frozen and freeze-dried foods can be bought from your pet shop, but they must always be defrosted or moistened before you give them to your fish. Canned foods help provide a balanced diet and come in a variety of forms, such as pellets, ranules, tablets, and flakes.

## Live Food

Piranhas like to eat plants, small animals, and microorganisms that either live in their tank or are introduced into it. Some piranhas enjoy mealworms, or black worms, and brine shrimps. Don't feed your piranhas live "feeder" fish such as goldfish. This can bring disease into your tank.

# How Much Food?

Piranhas have healthy appetites, and it is fun to watch them eat. Be warned, however, that they don't stop eating once they're full! Your fish should be able to eat all that you give them in two minutes; if it takes them more time than this, then you are probably over-feeding them. If you give your piranhas too much food, you will damage their health and increase the amount of waste produced in the tank. Give them less at the next mealtime.

Piranhas will gorge themselves if they are given the opportunity!

## Questions & Answers

**✴ What fresh meat and vegetables can I give my piranhas?**
You could offer them raw steak, fish chunks, seafood, potato, cucumber, spinach, and other green vegetables. Don't cook your piranhas' food, and always remember to wash your hands after feeding your fish.

**✴ What should I do with any leftover food?**
Always remove uneaten food with a net after your fish have finished eating. Uneaten food will rot and will make your tank smelly and unhealthy to live in.

**✴ What should I do if my piranha refuses to eat?**
This could be a sign of illness, so watch your piranha's general behavior. Offer something different next feeding time. If it still refuses food, get some expert advice.

## Tasty Treat

A piranha's body is covered in taste buds. As something floats past, piranhas can quickly decide whether it is worth chasing!

## How Often?

Young piranhas are growing and need feeding more often than fully-grown adults. Feed young piranhas once a day. Once they have reached adult size, you can feed them every other day. However old your fish, give them regular feedings. Small, regular meals are better than large infrequent ones.

# Cleaning Your Tank

The more you care for your tank, the healthier your piranhas will be. It is very important to clean your tank and change the water regularly. When your tank's biological filter is fully established, you will only need to change the water once a week.

## Removing Water and Waste

You should change between 10–15 percent of your tank water every week. Use a siphon with a nozzle to suck out dirty water from the tank. Place the other end of the siphon in a bucket. If you have an under–gravel filter, this is a good time to remove any waste blocking it up. Avoid moving the nozzle of the siphon around too much or you will stir up debris, which will be unpleasant for your fish.

When you siphon water out of your tank, put the nozzle on the tank bottom so that you remove waste as well as water.

## Don't "Top Off"

If some of your tank water has evaporated, you still need to do a water change. You shouldn't just top off the tank with fresh water. Remove 10 to 15 percent of the dirty water, and then fill the tank up to the original level. If you don't do this, toxic elements in the tank will get too strong and waste products will build up to harmful levels.

# Adding New Water

Make sure you have a bucket of warm, de-chlorinated tap water ready. The new water should be the same temperature as the water you are removing, so check this with a thermometer. Gently siphon the new water back into the tank, up to the level it was before.

# Be Safe

Your piranhas will be in your tank when you clean it, so an adult should always be present. Keep your hands out of the water when you use cleaning equipment, including siphons and algae scrubbers. Electrical equipment, such as mechanical filters, should be cleaned and checked by an adult. The electricity supply should be switched off when this is done.

# Algae

Algae is the green matter that lines your tank. It looks ugly. However, in small amounts, it is good for your piranhas, giving them extra oxygen. You can stop too much algae from growing in your tank by shielding it from direct sunlight (algae thrives on sunlight and will grow much faster in its presence) and by using the timer switches on your lighting.

## Questions & Answers

* **Why can't I pour new water directly into the tank?**
  If you pour new water into the tank straight from a bucket, it will disturb the gravel and decorations and upset your piranhas.

* **Should I clean the tank decorations?**
  No. Don't clean your decorations, or you may kill the good bacteria and stop the biological filter from working well.

* **Should I ever do a complete water change?**
  No. If you leave your tank for too long and then do a big water change, you change the water's chemistry drastically. This is bad for your piranhas. The more often you do your water changes, the smaller and easier they are to do.

Algae is a green plant that grows in any form of water. It takes in sunlight and gives off oxygen.

# Keeping Healthy Piranhas

Piranhas can get sick very suddenly. Signs of illness include gasping for air, floating or sinking, or behaving in other strange ways. Sick piranhas may refuse food or develop nasty spots, and their fins may even begin to rot. If you notice signs of illness, don't ignore them—get expert help right away.

## Prevention

The best way to keep piranhas healthy is to prevent illness in the first place. Keep your tank water clean and of good quality. Do regular checks, testing for acidity and for levels of calcium carbonate, nitrate, and oxygen. This ensures that the chemical balance of the water does not change. Your pet shop will sell testing kits and can show you how to use them.

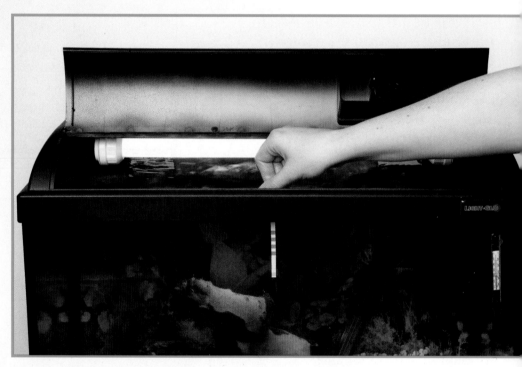

Water–testing kits change color when dipped in water to indicate the level of acidity in the tank.

## Stress Busters

Stress causes disease in fish, because it weakens their immune systems, making it harder to fight off illness. Stress can be caused by bad diet, poor water quality and incorrect water temperature. Remember that piranhas also need plenty of swimming space and shelter and will suffer stress if incompatible species are kept together in a tank.

# Getting Help

Successful treatment of piranha diseases depends on quick diagnosis. If one of your piranhas looks sick, get an adult to help you siphon some of the tank water into a bucket and transfer the fish into the bucket with a net. Take it to a vet or another fish expert. For example, you might go to the shop where you bought your fish.

# Hospital Tank

Keep your sick fish in a "hospital tank" while you give it medicine and allow it time to get better. This separation is good for all your fish. Left in the main tank, your sick piranha could be attacked, and the school could be infected by the sick piranha. It is a good idea to keep a spare tank and extra filtration and heating equipment for this purpose.

**A piranha wounded after an attack by its tank mates.**

## Questions & Answers

✳ **Should I ever give my piranhas medicine "just in case"?**
No. This will weaken their ability to fight infection when they really need to do so.

✳ **What should I do if one of my piranhas gets injured?**
If any of your piranhas is attacked by another member of the school, it will be weak and vulnerable to further, fatal attack. Get an adult to help put the injured fish in a hospital tank, and if the wound is infected, treat it with antibiotics from the vet.

✳ **When should I put my piranha back in its tank?**
When your piranha has recovered, it can go back in its old tank. Move it after feeding time, when the tank lights are off. Watch out for signs of aggression from the school toward the returning fish.

# Quarantine

If one of your piranhas dies and you want to add a new one to your school, buy another of the same species and size as the one you lost. Before you introduce the new fish to your aquarium, let it swim alone in your spare tank for about three weeks. This "quarantine" period will help you make sure that the new fish does not have an infectious disease.

# Caring for Your Aquarium

If you don't care for your aquarium properly, it won't look nice and it will be an unhealthy home for your piranhas. Get into a regular cleaning routine. Every time you feed your fish or clean your aquarium, check that your equipment is working properly. If you discover a problem, do something about it before it affects the health of your fish.

If you are worried about the health of one of your piranhas, put it in a separate tank for a while.

## Every Day

Every day when you feed your piranhas, check them for signs of illness and aggression toward each other. You may need to transfer any sick or injured fish to a "hospital" tank. Remember to take out any food that has not been eaten.

## Twice a Week

At least twice a week, get an adult to help you check that your heaters, pumps, and filters are working well. Remember to switch off electricity before checking equipment and repair or replace anything that is broken. Keep spares of important equipment, such as a heater, thermostat, filter, and air pump. These spares could save your piranhas' lives in an emergency.

# Once a Week

Once a week, change 10 to 15 percent of your tank water. You may need to remove algae from the walls of your tank with a long-handled scrubbing pad. Use a net to remove rotten waste, such as food or plant matter that has collected behind decorations or equipment. Ask an adult to clean the filters for you if they are dirty.

# Once a Month

Once every month, check all hoses, fittings, clamps, cords, lights, and other assorted tank equipment. Anything that is not working properly must be repaired or replaced immediately.

Use a long-handled scrubbing pad to clean the tank sides.

# Questions & Answers

✷ **What do I do if I spot a leak in my tank?**
This is a serious problem—leaks are not easy to fix permanently. You will almost certainly need to buy and set up another aquarium. To prevent any future leaks, make sure your tank is absolutely horizontal before you fill it with water.

✷ **Why do I need to check my tank so often?**
If you check your tank often, you will be able to deal with problems as they arise, before they become a danger to your piranhas' health.

✷ **Will it take long to check my tank?**
If you get into a regular routine, it doesn't take much time to check your tank. It's a good chance to admire your wonderful piranhas, too!

# Troubleshooting

If your water goes cloudy and begins to smell, there could be some rotten waste hidden somewhere. Your tank could also be too small, so there is too much waste for the filters. You may need to change the water and clean your filters more often. Whatever the reason for the problem, it must be solved before your fish get sick.

# Enjoy Your Hobby

Keeping piranhas can be a very rewarding experience. All it takes is a willingness to learn about your fish and their needs and plenty of time, patience, and enthusiasm. Good luck and have fun!

# Glossary

**acidity**
Acid is a sour substance, and acidity is the amount of acid that is present in something.

**air pump**
A device which pumps air into your tank to circulate the water and keep up levels of oxygen.

**algae**
Tiny green plants that grow inside your tank, lining the walls and decorations.

**antibiotics**
Medicine that is used to fight infection.

**bacteria**
Microorganisms that live in water, plants, and other living things.

**biological filter**
When natural bacteria and other microorganisms in the tank break down poisonous fish waste, making it less harmful.

**calcium carbonate**
A natural substance that can dissolve in water.

**captivity**
Living in an environment controlled by humans.

**chlorine/chloramine**
A chemical that can be added to tap water to clean it for human use. It is poisonous to piranhas.

**cycling**
The process of starting up a biological filter in an aquarium. Cycling can take four to eight weeks to complete.

**dechlorinate**
To remove chlorine and/or chloramine from tap water.

**evaporation**
The change from liquid to a gas. When water evaporates, it becomes water vapor or steam.

**filter**
A device or process that breaks down and removes harmful substances from the water in an aquarium.

**habitat**
A place where an animal lives.

**immune system**
The body's natural ability to fight off disease.

**microrganisms**
Living things that are so tiny they can only be seen through a microscope.

**nitrate**
A chemical that can dissolve in water.

**omnivore**
An animal that eats both meat and plants.

**quarantine**
A period of time during which a sick fish is separated from its tank mates to stop it from spreading an infectious disease.

**school**
A group of fish that swim together.

**species**
A group of one type of animal or plant.

**territory**
An area that belongs to a single individual.

**thermostat**
A device that keeps temperatures steady. A thermostat can be adjusted to make the temperature hotter or cooler.

**water circulation**
A moving flow of water. Piranhas need good water circulation in their tank to mimic conditions in the wild.

# Further Information

If you want to learn more about types of piranhas, buying piranhas, caring for piranhas, or if you would like to get involved in animal welfare, these are some helpful Web sites:

**Aquaria Central**
A free community of fish owners whose members share information about keeping fish.
Web site: www.aquariacentral.com

**First Tank Guide**
Information for people just getting started setting up their aquarium, including equipment and different kinds of fish.
Web site: www.firsttankguide.net

**Oregon Piranha Exotic Fish Exhibit**
Information for piranha keepers about a variety of species.
Web site: www.opefe.com

**People for the Ethical Treatment of Animals**
The largest animals rights group in the world. Contains information promoting the safety and responsible treatment of animals.
Web site: www.peta.org

**Piranha Fish**
Information on piranhas, including pictures and videos of the fish.
Web site: www.aquariumfish.net/catalog_pages/wild/piranhas.htm

**Piranha-Fury**
Piranha information site and discussion forum that includes information about buying and selling piranhas, feeding and nutrition, and much more.
Web site: www.piranha-fury.com

Note to parents and teachers: Every effort has been made by the publishers to ensure that these Web sites are suitable for children, that they are of the highest educational value, and that they contain no inappropriate or offensive material. However, because of the nature of the Internet, it is impossible to guarantee that the contents of these sites will not be altered. We strongly advise that Internet access is supervised by a responsible adult.

# Index